DAYJA BROWN

God Knows A Princess's Heart

The Purpose of the Book

The purpose of this book is not to tell a story but to tell a testimony of what the Lord has done for me. I have seen books that are good, but do not reflect or relate to what I've been through, so instead of just moving forward God gave me the assignment of authoring this book.

The Dedication

This book is dedicated to the King the Lord Himself, and my mother. Thank you, mom, for being my rock, and being there even when I did not show my gratitude. I am so glad that God has put you in my life. If it wasn't for you pushing me and warring for me in the spirit, I don't where I be.

Love,

Your baby girl

Table of Contents

Preface

Growing up there are so many ways that people want you to be, it is harder to stand out, and being chosen by God makes it harder. However, even though it is harder it is well worth it. Philippians 4:13 says, "I can do all things through Christ which strengthens me. "This scripture has stuck with me for years. Now that I am older, I understand it more, and He has been my strength. When I was sixteen God led me to start writing, and now He has given me the assignment to release my testimony. At first, I was like Lord "PLEASE GET SOMEBODY ELSE" but the Lord requires more, so he has given me an assignment to give more. This will not be a recounting of details, but hopefully it can connect to you in a way that you are able to relate. So, I pray that you receive what you need, and that God will speak to you throughout this book.

Chapter I

The Beginning Stage

From as far back as I can remember, my birth mother and I we were not in the best living conditions. We did not live like everybody else; we actually stayed in a hotel. My birth mother was going through a lot and raised me the best way she knew how. At this time, my birth mother became friends with someone that went to our church. One of the ladies that went to the church, adopted children. My birth mother decided to give me up for adoption. She began asking people at the church, "Hey, do you know if anyone is looking to adopt a child?" My birth mother's friend knew a family that was looking to adopt. The friend then asked them would they consider my mother and her situation, and they agreed. At this time, they were only going to keep me for a year to help my mother out, but God had other plans.

After a while we began to grow as a family, and they wanted to move forward with the adoption process. The way God moves is amazing, because they were going through the classes to prepare to adopt, and God brought me into their life. Sadly, after a while my adoptive father passed from cancer, and me and my mother had just each other. God had moved at the right time and put us together to be there for each other. I was still young and therefore unable to understand, but as I grew, I started to understand more and more why He had us together. My mother had signed the proper paperwork to adopt me. Since then, my mother and I have been together, even though we have our moments. God has been faithful to us and keeps us. My testimony is amazing because God's timing is always the right timing.

Chapter 2

Mother and I

My mother and I have been beside each other and around each other since the day I began living in her home. She's a "one call, that's all" person, and I never have to call or text twice. My mother is always going to know what is going on with me because I will tell her, or God will. When your parents are in God and in Christ, God gives them instructions concerning you. There was a season and a point where I did not really believe what my mother was saying because I thought she was acting on her emotions towards me. However, God had given her instructions concerning me, and it is amazing to see how God moves in our lives. Even when you do not want Him to move, He is still moving, so He has covered me through the tests of times, even through my mother's prayers. Her prayer was always for me to be protected by God, always follow His will, always serve Him, and love Him. She also desires for me to be in Christ, know who God is for myself, accept Him for myself, and walk in His life for myself.

So, yes, while I was still being rebellious (and let's put it out there – yes, I was rebellious and doing what I wanted to do), my mother was still praying on my behalf. I was still praying for myself as well. Eventually, God had to put me in check, put me in line, and I realized that my mother was actually just trying to protect me. She wanted me safe and sound, and to remember where I came from – to remember who created me and who is over my life.

There have been many times when I was convicted by God because of how I received what He was sending through my mother to me. He eventually broke me down. It was hard to hear, but it was God—talking to God would break me down there. He had to break me down to the point where I had to apologize and get back to the right standings, not only for my mother but also for myself.

During these challenging times, instead of releasing what I needed to release, I would hold it in and hold it against my mother for these things. These were issues I was going through, things I kept holding on to that I could have easily released to God and let Him fix and work on. So, I dealt with it (or at least I thought so), trying to keep everything away from my mother and keep it all in because I feared her reaction. But that is the person God put in my life to talk to, to go through to get knowledge and wisdom from, even though she didn't have to go through some of the same things I went through. He still put her in my life to help me and guide me in the right direction of where I need to go.

For this, I am forever grateful and know that God is with us. You may think that your parent doesn't understand, but don't forget they need grace and guidance from God too. It took me a long time to understand this because I wanted my mother to be able to help me, not realizing when she was hurt or needed time. This was selfish, and we don't think that way because we are used to parents always being there to guide us and help us. However, we are not perfect; we are human. So, with the help of God, grace, and forgiveness, we can get through it together.

Yes, my mother was tough on me, but it was for the better, and I can honestly thank God because I don't know where I would be without her. So, the next time you think it will never get better between you and your parent, remember that God is guiding you all and ask for His instructions on what to do. I want to give a big shout out to the queen herself, that calms me, who gives of her gifts, my pastor, and also my mother.

Chapter 3

Dancing for the King

In the body of Christ, everyone has their gifts that God has given us. The fun part is that sometimes God gives people more than one gift. One that God gave me is dance. Now, the thing is I have had a love and dislike (we should not use hate) relationship with dance. It all started with just doing the little flags in a dance for church on a special occasion. Then, the boys and girls would dance when we had youth days or events. I used to love it because it was something extra that I could do and move around. At the time, I didn't know that dancing for the Lord could help set the atmosphere, minister to people, and break some chains for yourself and others.

Younger me was like, "This is just a fun thing to do, and I get to wear a pretty dress and hair ribbon." However, it was more than that, but my young mind did not think of it that way. After a while, it became just another thing on the agenda for special occasions. After a while, we stopped, and it was something that just was. But who knew that it would be a ministry that God instilled in me? Years later, we transitioned to our new church family, and I was not prepared at all, I promise you. I screamed and hollered for like three Sundays straight; it was embarrassing. I know everyone was saying, "Girl, it is okay. Let's be real." Imagine knowing the people you are around and knowing their routine and having that change. The funny thing is, you know that God can use you, but you get scared when he is about to use you.

So, once I realized, "Okay, this is my new home," I started to get used to it. There was like one person that danced for the church, and we had talked to her and also the pastor. After that, I started dancing with her, and shortly after, some other people picked up. We started off doing group dances and working with them. Soon, I started doing solos. Keep in mind, around this time, I'm a teenager, and emotions are higher, and being worried about how people see me was a high priority, which is wrong. So, I was more focused on looking the best rather than letting God use me and letting loose in the spirit. It became a fight inside because I didn't want to let God down by looking crazy when He wanted me to trust Him and worship Him. I did not have a lot of faith and peace in this area. The crazy thing is faith and peace are a part of the spirit. Galatians 5:22-23 lists what the fruits of the spirit are, and there is one more fruit that I was having a hard time with, which was joy. It is supposed to be continuous in your life and ministry, but it was like a feeling of happiness. I was at a high in the spirit one minute, but the next minute, down. (Happiness is only temporary, but joy is everlasting, like God's love for us).

I would be on fire for dancing for the Lord, and then I would be upset because I couldn't figure out the moves or thought the moves, He gave me were embarrassing. Let's be truthful; that's how I was. Now, my mother was there to help and guide me, but I didn't want to listen to her. I would say I have to follow what my instructor was teaching me to do and ended up embarrassing myself because they wanted me to make up the moves, and I was still trying to figure out what God wanted me to do, and I'm still young at this time. So, it is better to have someone to help you cultivate your gift and hear from God, and my mother was just that (and still is). The whole time, God was giving my mom the guidance to be my teacher, but I was so hard-headed to take advice from her. I was thinking to myself, "This is not your lane, Mom," not knowing God gave her the guidance to help me.

Now, till this day, I laugh about it because as soon as I gave it all to God and followed His direction, I was doing so much better. In the past, I have dealt with low self-esteem with dance, even though the enemy tries to bring it up, but God conquers all. God was even downloading songs and dance moves into my mother for me, and I laugh about it because I say she wants to be a dance instructor so bad. I truly thank God that He used my mother to work with me and be patient with me even when I was being a brat.

Here is one thing that helps: don't take on the emotions or feelings of other people, especially when God gave you the gift. If He gave it to you, treat it how you would treat the best gift you ever got. Sometimes, after a while with gifts, we put them down until one day we randomly pick them back up. God gives us gifts that might come with challenges and make it hard, but it will always be worth it to give Him glory.

Now, I remember this story (well, really a lesson from God) like it was TODAY. We had been away at my new church for a while, and one of my church uncles wanted me to dance before he had to speak. I was about 14 or 15 around this time, so you know I wanted to be cool when I get around the other kids. I sat down and begin to talk to one of the new girls of the church. Keep in my mind I haven't met her, seen her, or knew about her. So, the whole time this girl was like, "I'm super nervous to talk, and scared to speak." I was thinking, since there was only a handful of kids, and mostly older people, if anyone messed up, they would say, "It's alright baby, take your time!" I was saying this not knowing what was truly going on. So, what happens? Because I was surrounded by someone who was operating in fear, guess who it fell on? You probably guessed it right, me. So, I start to freak out on the inside, and I didn't want it to show. Ironically enough, when it became time for the “scared” young lady to speak, she did without a single fault. I on the other hand had not internalized her fear and my nerves were all over the place. I’m crying at this point due to the fear upon me. This could’ve been avoided if I prayed it off, but I was so focused on not messing up the whole thing. The church was smaller, so you know I’m outside stretching, which was good at the time because I was crying like a big baby. Next thing I remember, all I could do was say I needed my momma.

The crazy thing is that if you know my momma, she ain't know "it's okay baby" type person. She is more of a "wipe them tears and get it together." I explained to her, and she reminded me that you let it come in; you have the power to cast these things down and move forward. Ever since then, I knew that my gift was a special gift that God gave me and that I needed to use. So now, I’m trying to stay in this gift and use it to glorify God even more. It’s a little hard because I’m not built like my size from high school, but I believe that God is going to make a way over time. The moral is don’t let your gift go away because of what people think. I’d rather do the craziest move He gives than settle for people's reactions. I've got more embarrassing stories that I can now laugh at because God was trying to get my attention, and being one of His chosen people is like a feeling that can't be taken, and I LOVE IT. Whatever gift God gave you, use it, and God will grow you in it. He will provide you with the strength you need and the endurance to keep going.

Chapter 4

Growing up in the Church

When I first started going to church, I was the type of child that did anything I was asked. I had no problem with it. I had no problem listening to people. I had no problem with new people. I had no problem doing what they asked me to do. But as I got older, sometimes people started to call me a goody two shoes, or the child that does everything, or the suck-up. I started to think about that real hard: "Am I actually doing those things?" Especially in church, when my mom always kept me there. People thought automatically that I was going to be one of them. They thought I would be a person who would not know how to stand up for myself. So, starting out, I did everything I was supposed to do. I even started praising God at a young age. I realized that the kids around me did not want to stand out, so when I wanted to speak and do things, I didn't because they didn't.

We would have meetings and Bible studies and they would ask people to speak up about what they learned, no one would stand up, including me. I just wanted to be like the cool kids. Now I started acting like a lot of people that I was around, I started thinking, well, maybe if I just fit in it's going to work. I did not have a lot of friendships in church. I wanted to build friendships, but it did not work as planned. I started to do stuff and then think, "why would you do this?" For example, I would have candy and I would just give them all of it and it still would not work like I had planned. One day I gave all my candy out and did not realize it until the end of service. I was confused. I got frustrated, so I just got to the point where, I asked, "what am I supposed to do?" My mother was big on not trying to fit in. "You are not supposed to fit in." She has been saying that ever since I was little, "Yeah, you're saying that, but you're not experiencing what I am." My mother went through most of those experiences, but sometimes when it is coming from a parent, you don't want to hear it because we know that the parent is mostly right, but we don't want them to be.

I remember one incident at church where I was with my actual friend, but I still desired friendship from other girls; we were all sitting, and because they treated me so bad, I felt like if I treated somebody else bad, I would feel better, and they would let me fit in. Me and this other girl (that I was using as a target) were cool, but I decided to bully her. I wanted to be all tough because I was shown that in order to fit in you must be on top and tear others down. The kids started laughing and everything, but I felt so bad. My mom was confused as to why I was acting like this. I finally broke, I told her, how I was being treated. I got picked on because I'm do the right thing. If I do this and they tell me to do this, it is a joke. There was a long conversation about it, and my mom spoke with their parents. Everybody was upset and asking about me telling my mom. They asked, "Is this what we doing?" I did not understand how they referred to my mom as "auntie" but did not treat her child right. I was basically their cousin.

There was so much going on, however it all worked out in the end, because I grew out of that phase. I used to let it hurt me, but I know how I am, and God knows me and that's all that really matters. I remember we used to sing *I'm Walking Authority* by Donnie McClurkin. The whole song was about how we are adopted into the family (the body of Christ), and that God gave me the right to be here. So, it's crazy that I can look back and laugh, because even though I am wondering about why I let that get to me. I know now that you don't have to be friends with everybody. God was testing me and showing me that this was a season I would have to just walk through. I have forgiven those young ladies and I love them until this day; besides we were just kids.

Chapter 5

Goody Two Shoes: Reality Check

Many may think that it is so easy to be a good girl and you never have to go through anything. Whoever said that was completely wrong. I was baptized at the age of 12, I was persistent. I was on the usher board, the choir, and I was doing everything. Around the age of 13, I got to the point where I started to have an identity crisis. In this case, you don't know who you want to be, who you want to hang with, or what you want to do. It was affecting me mentally. So, what I started to do was channel what people were doing and channeling the stuff they had going on. I thought this was the best way for me to process things, however it did not work. It does not matter how you change how you act people in the world, people will always know when God is in you.

I used to think that I can hide being the God-fearing girl, but nope. God made it to where people saw the God in me. I had friends around this time, and I watched their lifestyles and always tried to relate. I tried to carry their burdens. I should have tried to witness to them and let them know I had been there where they are, but sadly I chose to still fit-in. My witnessing and questioning of their situations could've helped. I was supposed to be the influencer in the situation, instead I decided to dim my light and not be the beacon. As a young person it is hard sometimes to be that light for people, because it causes you to be set-apart, which is not a bad thing, but it feels like it is. Matthew 5:14 says that "Ye are the light of the world. A city that is set on a hill cannot be hid."

God has made some of us lights that can't be hidden but we try so hard to hide it. Now during high school, I started to go through the growing pains, and they are nothing to be played with. I had to go through the pressing and the shaping process to get to this point. Now freshman year started out smooth, I was still getting bullied, but it was not the biggest problem. I started to fall back in my academics, and it was a lesson to learn. My teachers always told my mom that I was smart enough to be in the higher classes, but I was still trying to fit in. In eighth grade, we had to take placement test to get in the classes we desired.

I tried to outsmart my mom and the school, but it backed fired so hard. I remember the day like it was yesterday, I had gone all week and passed all my placement test except math. I knew if I failed that one it just meant I did not go to a higher math class, it also meant I would have to repeat my current math. This was a bad decision, but I wanted to fit in and that was important to me at this time. As hard as I tried to fail, I actually passed. Trying to fit-in was never going to work. One thing about God is that he is always going to put you in a situation of being uncomfortable so you can grow. If you can say that you never experienced anything while walking with God then that may be your journey, however when it comes to me. He put me through some hard times, and this was one of them. It's like I had to pick between my beliefs or having friends. The crazy thing is God will make it to where the people I wanted to act like would reject me as a friend, it hurt but it was for my good. I got to the point that I said okay let me stay to myself, but I did not accept it all the way.

As the year continued, I was still trying to win brownie points with them, but it did not work. At the time I had two best friends that I'd known for years. I was also in JROTC and my instructor was very hard on me, because he knew that I stood out. However, my mindset at the time led me to believe he was coming at me, and trying to make everything hard, but God also has a way of using the people around me. Not only him, all of my teachers would say that I had leadership characteristics, but I would fall into trying to be cool with the wrong crowd. I used to think they didn't understand, but they were on the outside looking in. The whole time I was thinking that I needed to keep a lot of people around me that had a popular reputation. Which was not what I needed God knows what you need even when you don't want to accept that you might have to walk alone.

In 1Chorinthians 15:33 it says, "Be not deceived: evil communication corrupts good manners." This is the truth, because you make think "I'm still the same person," but that is not the case." You take on some of the ways they act to fit in, and it doesn't turn out for the best. God had to really deal with me on this and get me to be in the light he called me to walk in. By senior year I was cool with my few friends, but it should have been less than that. See I had friends that would talk about me and give advice that would turn me away from my destiny. Eventually God had to remove them his way it hurt, but it made me better. I tried to hold onto some, but it took a decision that God gave me to choose the right way. I still pray for those friends, but I know that I was only supposed to be in their life for a season. I'm glad I have my faithful few, and that's all I need.

A great woman (my mother) reminded me that sometimes you are put in people's lives to pour into them only. Now you would think that senior year would be a breeze because all of the work had been done, but things got even crazier. The enemy was coming at me left and right. I was being bullied still and trying to fight back, but things were just getting worse. Afterwhile I just hit the bully with kindness, and it was like the situation changed overnight. Now I'm not saying we became besties, but I know that God can fix any problem that you bring him. Even after the bullying I thought it was over, but even more test and trials appeared. I needed help with my healing and deliverance. There were things I held deep down that wanted to come out. I was trying to fight those issues as well. I was dealing with relationship heartbreaks that I could have avoided, and the trauma I had stored away. Lots of people don't talk about this subject in the black community, but I fell into depression. It was hard to think that I had fallen this far. I had an explosion. I tried to express myself, but I didn't have the right words to say. I was trying to ask myself what was going on with me, but I didn't have the correct delivery. I felt like I had to turn to just holding a lot in and just let it settle, and not worry about it. Sometimes when we hold stuff in we can get in a place of not getting the help and healing we need. Mostly in the African American culture therapy is mostly frowned upon. We are strong people especially the women, and we believe that we can let it roll over our shoulder. Most of the time we are making it worse, by not getting the help.

By this time, I was trying to figure out who I was. The good thing about God is that we come to him for a way to be fixed from being broken, and not come to him when we already are fixed. So, all the test and trials are helping to work for our good. Remembering Psalms 30:5, I know from my experience that joy will come in the morning light, especially when you are doing the work of God and following what he needs you to. Looking back there is a lot of trauma that I've experienced, but it is my testimony. When I was younger someone close touched me inappropriately and told me not to tell my mother. My mother taught me that nobody was supposed to touch me in that way. However, imagine wanting to tell someone, but you're still in shock that this is happening at the hands of someone close to you. He would make me do things to give him pleasure, and when someone would come around, he would tell me not to say anything. This was hard for me. I was confused and wondered, "Why me?" I cried because I knew that it would break my mother's heart. It was a hard time, but even though I was going through it, God was there. One day he touched me, I yelled. My mom heard me and asked what happened. I then told her, he poked me. He said that it was a joke. Me being so afraid I stood in fear wondering, "What do I need to say?" I was afraid of telling the truth and what would happen. I said I forgave him but did not truly forgive him; there is a difference. I would think he would see where he was wrong, but he didn't. He was mad at me for yelling and telling, and I didn't understand why. I begin to think like I did something wrong. My mother often asked if I told her everything that was going with me at any time, and I would avoid that question.

At one point it really hurt my feelings. I wondered why he had so much hatred towards me. I felt like he should have understood that it was hurting me. I spent a while thinking it was my fault because I wanted to tell the whole truth, but I didn't have the guts to do so. It was never my fault. My mom continued to ask if I told her everything, and I still avoided that question. The truth is the incidents continued for a little while, but mom did not know. I never revealed everything to my mother, and I suffered tremendously and battled in my mind due to the whole experience. I felt that I had to give my body to others in order to be loved. It was all mental. Who knew being touched inappropriately and battling in my mind, would push me into God's presence? I began to blame my mother although she did not know what was going on. I realized I needed to ask her for forgiveness. I asked God to forgive me for holding that against her and putting her in that spot. I had to come to her completely, and tell her everything, because I knew if I didn't then I would be carrying unforgiveness in my heart. We talked and prayed about it, and I know God was shifting things for us at this time.

God has revealed to me that I don't come in agreement with the hurt but grow from it. He also told me what I would receive in a relationship. Like, He would bring somebody up to my level where they have to ensure it and actually see where I was coming from, and actually know what I need to do and fall in God's lineup. At first, I didn't feel that about myself, so I got into relationships and suffered late-night conversations that were very sexual, and the people I was dating at the time were just looking at me for my body.

I was looked at as a body count, and I think that hurt the most at times. This became a place where I had to honestly trust God and do what He needed. Also, I had to ask for forgiveness for my mindset. I asked for forgiveness for thinking lower of myself, even forgiving the person that hurt me. I believe that God is working on him and his life because we have to realize we never know what somebody really experiences, and God knows all, so He has the last say. I even had to ask my mother for forgiveness because my anger would come out towards her, and I was hurt.

When I began to go deeper in God, He started showing me myself and showed me what I needed to work towards. So, the weight I was carrying around was lifted, and I felt joy and peace. It was not an easy process; a lot of tears were shed, and words came out that I had to repent for, but God still gave me grace and allowed me to make it through this. I never thought I would come out of the hole, but He came down and got me out because He knew what I needed.

Chapter 6

Don't Tilt Your Crown Princess

We have to understand that we do not have to lower our standards and ways to be loved. However, the human part of us does it because we think we have to do it. Let me tell you something; I was trying to fit into the wrong relationship and the wrong crowd. Now, in middle school, you know how your mom told you not to date because you were not allowed to, well, there is a reason for that. I started dating this dude behind my mother's back (that's called rebellion WARNING: If you can't handle the consequences, do not do it).

So, this dude told me he liked me and buttered me up and was telling me I was the world but could not give me the world in reality. His friends would laugh at me because at this time I had cut my hair and had an afro, and it was a little short. So, I just brushed it off. Now, the Lord knows me and would not let me go down like that, so I got caught every time talking to him, and my mom would tell me to stay away from him. The final time she talked to my counselor, and she talked to his parents, this dude told all of his homeboys, and they spread it like wildfire. I was embarrassed, but now I know it was for my good. The same boys that were laughing at me that were supposed to be his homeboys were the same ones trying to get my number. The boy kept coming up to me and trying to get with me, but he would play me every time, and when I said I'm done, he thought I was joking. I hope he knows I meant it. I got rid of the number and the socials. The moral of the story is don't put yourself where you do not belong, and also, your parents hear from God, and He gives instructions concerning you. I thank God even after the relationships; he told me to pray for my future husband. Yes, people might say you're young, how can He show you that? All I have to say is He is God, and I TRUST IN HIM.

Chapter 7

Depression to Diamonds

Listen, the stereotype for African Americans is to just brush things off and move on. When you think of depression, you think of a deep, dark place that hurts and makes you feel like you've lost it all and cannot bring your head back above water. Now, I would say that going through it, I THANK GOD THAT IT DID NOT KEEP ME BOUND. After my last relationship, I completely went through it because I was not healed. I went through therapy and deliverance and felt a weight lifted, but at some point, I felt like I was missing more.

So, I did not want to get out of bed. I was just going through the motions. I went to work, school, and just kept doing what I was supposed to do. Keep in mind that I was in my senior year, so this was around prom and graduation time, and it's supposed to be the best thing. However, when I went through deliverance and was releasing some things, then God removed people and stuff from me to keep me on the right path. I realized the guy I was dating was not for me, and it was hard to understand. Keep in mind the signs were there; everything was an argument; he didn't have my back. His friends were people that have tried to talk to me or were an ex that became his friend just to spite me. So, they always put their two cents in, and I felt like I was the only one to defend myself, and it was crazy.

There was a lot going through my mind, and keep in mind that he was not the best-looking fella, so I was like I just got played. The same friends that were talking about us being together were the main ones trying to talk to me. I don't know if they missed all the stuff that was caused, but let's be honest now. So, I tried to keep my head up, but I was barely floating, and the hurt was deep. I was already going through so much mentally (I didn't need to be in a relationship at the time), so my heart was hurting bad.

Then I had school, track, and the teachers being messy, so they were asking questions and it would get awkward. I was crying like every five seconds, and it was not because I got broken up with; it's the fact that I got played, and when God told me to let him go, I thought I had to do the right thing by giving him a chance. That was the wrong way to go. If God tells you to let go or end it, just do it, save yourself a lot of heartbreak.

See the whole time, the specific boy knew what I was dealing with and going through, and he was not encouraging or trying to be there. Both of my best friends were there, and they made sure every time that I cried, they would remind me of who God said I was. I also had some family friends that I would confide in. Now after all this, right before prom, graduation, and the celebrations, I would give up? NOOOOO. I got back into prayer, and you would think that I wouldn't want to pray for this dude, but I did. Not only did I pray for him, God had me pray for his future and his future wife and children.

Now at first, I was like after what he just did, he didn't deserve it, but that is not my call to make. So eventually, I got back to being the princess God called me to be. I started eating better, coming to track practice early, and running the laps instead of just doing it. I was making sure my grades were squared away and all credits were done. Then prom rolled around now, I was hurt but not hurt enough to sit out before prom. Now as I sit here and read this to myself, I can laugh and remember the hard parts but have peace because God said He's with me and carried me.

Chapter 8

Not the End of the Testimony: The Princess Era

I thank God for what He is doing in my life, and I will never give up. After four years of writing, I get to see everything that I went through, and my growth in Christ. I know that few are called, and you still have to choose the call. I will never let go and will keep going. This is the start of something new. I pray that it reaches that one person or group that feels all hope is lost. I want to use my testimony to glorify God and share His goodness. If my 16-year-old self can see what God has done... FULL TEARS AND PRAISE TO GOD. The process was hard, but the purpose is well worth it. So, to whoever reads this testimony, they will see the goodness of God and be encouraged. The great thing is I don't know where He is taking me next; I'm just enjoying the ride and having faith in His words. Who knows where He will take me, but I pray that His will be done. Every tear, heartache, and growing pain brought me this far.

Remember CHOOSE TO BE CHOSEN.

Here are some affirmations you can say to remind you (young ladies) that you are his Princess.

1.I'M PRETTY

2.I'M LOVED

3.I'M GOD'S DAUGHTER

4.I HAVE A PURPOSE AND DESTINY

5.I WILL NOT FAIL

6.MY PROCESS IS NOT TO HURT ME, BUT TO GROW ME.

7.I WILL BE THE LIVING TESTIMONY

8.I WILL OVERCOME EVERY OBSTACLE

9.GOD CREATED ME IN HIS IMAGE

10. I WILL DO THE WILL AND WORK OF GOD.

See there are so many ways you can hype yourself up and remind yourself God has you. Never let go of his promises because he always fulfills them. I pray whatever you're carrying you will birth it out to glorify God. Always know that nothing is in vain, and you are worth it all.

The time 11:56 on September 7,2023. I put my last words in this book for it to be complete. I can smile, and I can wait for you to take this journey with me. There may be more books to come…stay tuned.

Love,

A Princess in the Kingdom of God.

About the Author

Dayja Brown, a 20-year-old author and college student, was born in Montgomery, Alabama, and currently resides in Prattville. She is pursuing a degree in Computer Information Systems at Trenholm State Community College and serves as an ambassador for the school. Dayja also works as an innovative instructor at EDfarm, teaching coding to middle school students in Montgomery.

A dedicated member of Hearts Evolved Ministries, Dayja attends the home church led by Pastor Barbara Brown. Through her personal testimony and steadfast faith, Dayja has discovered the transformative power of sharing her experiences. In her writing, she delves into the depths of her journey, using her unique voice to narrate stories of resilience, growth, and the constant presence of God in her life.

Dayja's literary journey is a testament to the strength found in vulnerability as she fearlessly navigates life's challenges with the guiding light of her faith. Her work is characterized by an authentic exploration of her own experiences, aiming to connect with readers on a profound level. Through her words, Dayja creates a space for reflection, healing, and hope, anchored in the belief that God's grace is a constant source of inspiration.

As a dedicated young author, Dayja Brown is committed to using her testimony and faith to encourage and empower others through her written works.

www.ingramcontent.com/pod-product-compliance
Lightning Source LLC
Chambersburg PA
CBHW040114150726
48005CB00013B/1698
* 9 7 9 8 8 6 9 2 0 9 8 2 5 *